Greater Than a To Manhattan New York USA

50 Travel Tips from a Local

Amy Alexander Sylvestre

Order Information: To order this title please email lbrenenc@gmail.com or visit
GreaterThanATourist.com. A bulk discount can be provided.

Cover Template Creator: Lisa Rusczyk Ed. D. using Canva.
Cover Creator: Lisa Rusczyk Ed. D.
Image: https://pixabay.com/en/new-york-skyline-new-york-city-city-668616/

Lock Haven, PA
All rights reserved.
ISBN: 9781549564468

>TOURIST

Amy A. Sylvestre

BOOK DESCRIPTION

Are you excited about planning your next trip?

Do you want to try something new?

Would you like some guidance from a local?

If you answered yes to any of these questions, then this Greater Than a Tourist book is for you.

Manhattan by Amy Sylvestre offers the inside scoop from a local on the most famous borough of New York City. Most travel books tell you how to sightsee. Although there's nothing wrong with that, as a part of the Greater than a Tourist series, this book will give you tips from someone who lives at your next travel destination. In these pages, you'll discover local advice that will help you throughout your trip.

Travel like a local. Slow down and get to know the people and the culture of a place. By the time you finish this book, you will be eager and prepared to travel to your next destination.

Amy A. Sylvestre

TABLE OF CONTENTS

12. Try China Town Soup Dumplings

13. Take A Picnic in the Park

14. Enjoy Cupcakes & Banana Pudding

15. Find Cheap Eats

16. Navigate Times Square

17. Eat REAL NY Pizza

18. Find the Secrets of The Plaza Hotel

19. Be A Local At The Street Fairs

20. Don't Skip Lincoln Center

21. Bring Cash to Try the Best Street Food

22. Don't Buy The Expensive Stuff

23. Visit The Highline

24. Don't Miss The Best Burgers & Shakes

25. Eat A Meal On The Hudson

26. Remember In Lower Manhattan

27. Bike Along The Hudson

28. Visit Top Of The Rock Or Empire State Building

29. See A Movie In Bryant Park

30. Try Some Spice With Indian Food Under the Lights

31. Take the Staten Island Ferry

Amy A. Sylvestre

Our Story

Notes

DEDICATION

This book is dedicated to

my brave heart warrior son, Hudson, named for the beautiful

Hudson River where I fell in love with his daddy.

July 17, 2015-March 20, 2016

Amy A. Sylvestre

ABOUT THE AUTHOR

Amy Sylvestre is a wife, mom and writer from North Carolina. Amy fell in love with her husband walking through the streets of New York and was engaged in Central Park. Amy enjoys time with her family, a good book, the beach and quoting the show, "*Friends*." After completing her Master's Degree focused on International Relations, she has ended up living in several major cities in the United States. She has traveled around much of Europe and India. She also spent two summers in South Africa and six months in France. Amy lived for over five years on the upper west side of Manhattan and she completely agrees with Zoe McLellan's feelings when she said, "I lived in New York for a while and miss it likes it's a person. There is no other city like in the world!" Amy misses the pulse, pace and most of all, the people of The City!

Amy A. Sylvestre

HOW TO USE THIS BOOK

The Greater Than a Tourist book series was written by someone who has lived in an area for over three months. The goal of this book is to help travelers either dream or experience different locations by providing opinions from a local. The author has made suggestions based on their own experiences. Please do your own research before traveling to the area in case the suggested places are unavailable.

Amy A. Sylvestre

FROM THE PUBLISHER

Traveling can be one of the most important parts of a person's life. The anticipation and memories that you have are some of the best. As a publisher of the Greater Than a Tourist book series, as well as the popular 50 Things to Know book series, we strive to help you learn about new places, spark your imagination, and inspire you. Wherever you are and whatever you do I wish you safe, fun, and inspiring travel.

Lisa Rusczyk Ed. D.

CZYK Publishing

Amy A. Sylvestre

WELCOME TO > TOURIST

Amy A. Sylvestre

INTRODUCTION

New York City is made up of five boroughs and the most famous one is called *Manhattan*. Just being in this amazing city can lift your spirits, challenge you to dream bigger dreams and expose you to people you wouldn't meet otherwise. The locals know that the crowds, noise and hassles of big city living are worth it. They know where to go to find a respite from the chaos that comes with being in this *city that never sleeps*. Visiting New York will allow you to see cultures from all over the world on one small city island. You will find historical sites, people from every walk of life and make lasting memories as you soak up the city streets. Explore on foot as much as you can. Meet some locals. Eat delicious food. Hopefully you will understand what Tom Wolfe felt when he said, "One belongs to New York instantly, one belongs to it as much in five minutes as in five years."

Take advice from me and instead of waiting in long lines at tourist destinations, explore like a local and walk away from your trip feeling a bit more like a New Yorker. Lindsey Kelk compares two of the most interesting cities saying, "People go to LA to "*find themselves*," they come to New York to become *someone new*." My hope for you is just that. Grow and expand your horizons as you travel this life-changing city. Plan to come back again and again. Claim a piece of the city for yourself and share it with others. Don't let this trip be limited to simply just *seeing* all this famous island has to offer but also a time to grow yourself, your worldview and your dreams for your future. Remember, *if you can make it here, then you can make it anywhere.*

Amy A. Sylvestre

1. Don't Miss The Park

While Manhattan offers so many amazing places to see, Central Park is at the very top of my list. Be sure to stroll through *The Mall* (also known as *Poet's Walk*) and enjoy the forever present saxophone player near the *Bandshell*. Take photos at the famous *Bethesda Fountain*. Have Brunch at the *Boat House*. Picnic on the *Great Lawn* and visit *Turtle Pond*. Look out over the park from the Castle and take a walk from East to West around the *Jacklyn Onassis Reservoir*. Try to get lost in *The Ramble*. Take a six mile bike ride around the loop or take nap in *Sheep's Meadow*. If you are traveling with your children, there are playgrounds near entrances at West 59th Street and West 66th Street. Don't be afraid to wander around the park. You can't get lost if you know this local tip. The number on the lamp posts will tell you the nearest street. For example, if the posts reads W10109, you are near West 101st street or if it reads E7901, you are closest to East 79th street. So, go explore and don't worry about getting lost!

2. Stay On The Upper "Best" Side

Every neighborhood in Manhattan has its own personality and draws different types of New Yorkers and visitors. You will find that each one offers unique qualities and diversities. Teju ColeIf explains that, "Each neighborhood of the city appeared to be made of a different substance, each seemed to have a different air pressure, a different psychic weight: the bright lights and shuttered shops, the housing projects and luxury hotels, the fire escapes and city parks." You can ask most local New Yorkers which neighborhood is the best to visit, they will tell you the reasons why their neighborhood surpasses the others. I guess I am no different. The *Upper West Side* offers amazing restaurants, museums and is more family friendly than many neighborhoods in Manhattan. Its borders are Central Park and

Riverside Park along The Hudson River. Some major subway stops are West 66th Street, West 72nd Street and West 96th Street. If you have a choice of where to stay on the island, be sure to choose The Upper "Best" Side.

3. Travel to Manhattan From Airports

Navigating any big city can be very overwhelming and New York is no different. It is expansive with many modes of transportation. You can fly into JFK, La Guardia or Newark airports. If you fly into JFK or Newark, I would suggest taking the AirTrain. From JFK you will then take the Long Island Railroad and then get off at Penn Station. From the Newark AirTrain, take the NJ Transit. From Penn Station you can take the MTA subway or buses anywhere in Manhattan. If you are traveling with several people, you can split the taxi fare for similar costs as the trains and subway. If you fly into La Guardia, the easiest way to Manhattan is a taxi and is more reasonably priced than the fares from JFK and Newark. You can also take the M25 bus but it fills up quickly with people, their luggage and this trip will likely give you a few more gray hairs.

4. Don't Get Lost: Subway and Buses

You will need a MTA card to travel on the subway and you can purchase it in most all subway stops. If you find a stray one on the ground, pick it up. It might have money on it! At the very least, it will save you the cost of the card. The good thing to note is that you can use the same card on the buses. Otherwise, to take a bus, you will need exact change. Most of the subway trains run North-South, so if you need to travel East-West, you may need to take a bus. If you are staying for several days, you will likely save money if you buy an unlimited pass. If you plan to stay in one or two neighborhoods on your visit, you can simply add money to your MTA card as you need it. Be sure to pay attention to if the you are taking a local or an express train. A local train will stop every ten to fifteen blocks and the express train will skip many stops to make the commute shorter. Keep in mind that on weekends and holidays, trains will often only run local which means it will take you longer to get to your destination. The 1,2,3 trains are more frequent than the B,C trains. Obviously prepare to be closer to strangers than you'd prefer, know where you are getting off before you get on and keep your belongings close. If you are confused, find a local. Even after a year of using the subway, it is easy to get a little confused or turned around. If you are lucky, you will get to enjoy subway performers on the train. There are always performers in the Times Square stop. Be sure to wander around underground at West 42nd street and see some amazing talent! Some subway stops have little shops and restaurants as well. You can easily download the subway map application to help you not end up in Brooklyn. It happens to the best of us.

5. Take A Short Trip And Pick Only The Best

You can spend many years in New York and not see all the major sites. I read once that it would take over twenty years to try all the restaurants in New York. If you are going for just a few days, pick your top favorites sites and plan ahead when you will visit each place. It will take you longer than you think to get around the city. You will likely enjoy your visit more if you aren't exhausted and annoyed by all the challenges that come with city travel. To hit the highlights, I would suggest the Brooklyn Bridge, Battery Park, Times Square, Central Park, Grand Central Station and a walk along The Hudson River.

6. Seeing All Of Columbus Circle

You will know you have arrived in Columbus Circle by the beautiful silver globe of the world outside of Trump Tower and the huge statue of Columbus. In this area you can get some serious shopping done in the mall. There are major name brand shops as well as a Whole Foods grocery store underground. You will find street performers, carriage rides, and a convenient subway stop at the entrance of Central Park. The best way to see all of Columbus Circle is having brunch or dinner in the top floor restaurant, Robert. You will see spectacular views of the park, Columbus Circle and Central Park South!

7. Visit Museums And The Bronx Zoo Free or Cheap

If you are like me, it is important to stretch a dollar while traveling. Saving your budget on food, entry fees and getting around the city will allow you to spend your money elsewhere. One place you can save significantly might surprise you. Many museums, and even the Bronx Zoo, have a "pay what you wish" policy. You simply make a donation of your choice and enter the site. The Modern Museum of Art (MoMA) is free on many Friday nights but prepare to wait in line. The Museum of Natural History and the Metropolitan Museum of Art has a suggested adult entry prices but the policy is that you can pay whatever donation you decide. Do a quick search online to find details for other free museums hours in NYC.

8. Map Out the Sites

Because there is so much to see in Manhattan, I would suggest visiting sites in groups based on location and subway stops. Instead of seeing something in Harlem and then riding the train all the way downtown, save yourself some time by mapping out your days. Here's an example day: Take the one train downtown. You can see the 9/11 Memorial and Museum, St. Paul's Chapel and Wall Street all by walking. You can end your day by taking a walk over the Brooklyn Bridge and having pizza at Grimaldi's. If you are ambitious, before you cross the bridge, you can go see Lady Liberty from Battery Park. By grouping your site visits together, you will save so much time and avoid waiting for trains and buses. You can enjoy the Big Apple the best way: on foot!

9. Enjoy Family Style Italian

There are many amazing restaurants with authentic cuisine in New York. In little Italy, you will find lots of carb lovers Italian cuisines but my favorite authentic Italian food is served family style at *Carmine's*. Be sure to go hungry and with friends. The portions are huge and the bread is divine! Be sure to order the *lemon butter chicken with penne* but save room for their famous dessert called, "*The Titanic*." You can search for pictures of this dessert online. Prepare to be amazed! If you are seeing a show in the Theater District, you could plan to have dinner at the Times Square *Carmine's*. There are several additions locations around the city but my favorite is on Broadway on the Upper West Side.

10. To Go Or Not To Go

Should you go to New York? Honestly, that is not the question at hand. You should go! But, it is a big consideration on whether to go to the Statue of Liberty and Ellis Island. I know that most people would think that seeing these two sites are a must see but hear me out. While seeing these historically famous sites is a must for your lifetime, if you are only in New York for two or three days, you need to consider a few things. Going on the ferry and touring these two islands makes for wonderful conversations, photos and memories. It is worth it if you have the time and energy. But, you must plan to spend at least half a day completing the tours. I would also suggest booking your tickets online. Prepare for a security check and lines very similar to TSA at the airport. You will also want to budget enough time to see all that Battery Park has offer while in this area of Manhattan.

Amy A. Sylvestre

"Once you have lived in New York and it has become your home, no place else is good enough."

John Steinbeck

Amy A. Sylvestre

11. Splurge Here

If you're lucky, you will find yourself in Manhattan during restaurant week. You can order a multi-course meal in some of the finest restaurants for under $40. If you miss this week of reduced prices, I would suggest splurging at *Delmonico's* for the best steak you will ever eat! You can also have lunch at *Jean Georges* in the Trump Tower on the Upper West Side. You will need a reservation at both locations and lunches will be cheaper than dinner. You might blow your food budget for a few days but you will remember these meals for years to come.

12. Try China Town Soup Dumplings

Whether you are trying soup dumplings for the first time or this is a staple in your diet, you will not regret a visit to Joe's Shanghai in China Town. Be sure to take a walk around the shops in this extremely unique neighborhood. You will certainly feel transported overseas. If you are an adventurous eater, you can venture through the grocery markets and buy live frogs from a bucket for your dinner! Bon appetit!

13. Take A Picnic in the Park

Let's face it, New York City is very expensive. One way to cut the cost and live a like a local is to grab a sandwich and a few side items and then head to the park. There are many places to enjoy a laid back picnic but I would suggest a stroll through *The Mall (Poet's Walk)* and then settling down in *Sheep's Meadow* for a relaxing time with friends. Plus, some of the best photographs of the city are taken here. If it is Sunday afternoon or evening, please do yourself a favor and go see the roller skater dancers near *The Mall*. It is unreal! Riverside Park is a lovely place for a quiet picnic away from the hustle and bustle of city life. If you are downtown, Washington Square Park is an eclectic neighborhood of locals, visitors and students from New York University. The park features the beautiful historic arch that resembles the Arc de Triomphe in Paris. It was built in 1892. You will also find one of the oldest trees in Manhattan in this area near the Arch. I hope you enjoy your picnic lunch outdoors in any of these fantastic city parks.

14. Enjoy Cupcakes & Banana Pudding

There are so many amazing bakeries in Manhattan that it can be overwhelming deciding where to indulge your sweet tooth. After a day of walking the city streets, I would suggest awarding yourself with a delicious cupcake or unbelievable banana pudding from *Magnolia Bakery*. These cupcakes were made famous by the HBO series, *Sex and the City*. There are several Manhattan locations but you will find the original location is in the West Village. You won't regret these yummy rewards. Enjoy!

15. Find Cheap Eats

In Manhattan, you can easily spend the bulk of your travel budget on just feeding yourself. The variety of restaurants is overwhelming and even a simple meal could be significantly more expensive than what you pay in your hometown. If you don't plan ahead and then you might find yourself starving in higher end restaurant where you could easily spend $60 on a pizza and $25 for a burger. It has happened to me. Here are a few places to check out. Don't be scared of street cart food! Try a hot dog from Gray's Papaya. Grab a *slice*. Get an ice cream treat from a Mr. Softie truck. As suggested in another tip, stop by Trader Joe's and then have a picnic in the park. Don't buy drinks from the carts next to the tourists spots. You will pay nearly double! I will suggest eating at places that are unique to New York and not food chains. You can grab McDonald's and Chipotle back home. Venture out and get a local meal.

16. Navigate Times Square

Prepare for sensory overload when you come up out of the subway in the middle of Times Square! No matter what time of day you choose to take in this city neighborhood, be ready for an enormous amount of people as well as the bright lights and the noises from traffic, car horns and crowds. There will locals trying to get to their normal subway stop. There will be street performers of all types. There will be tour groups blocking the side walk as they try to figure out where to go next. Prepare to be attacked with requests to purchase bus tours and comedy show tickets. Even with all of the chaos, there is a beauty to Times Square. I was in this area almost every day for over five years. I had a love/hate relationship with Times Square as I would make my way through the crowds day after day. There is great people-watching and shops to check out but you have to deal with lost tourists and all that comes with such big crowds in just a few blocks. One great little tip for your Manhattan visit is if you are planning to see Grand Central Station, going from West 42nd Street is a convenient solution.

Go into a Times Square subway station and take the S (Shuttle) train over to East 42nd Street. This shuttle train runs between these two stops, back and forth, east and west, all day long. Also, there is a food court in the downstairs of Grand Central with a variety of restaurants. I'll also share with you a little local secret that you can find at the *Whispering Gallery* next to the Oyster Bar as you go down the ramp to the food court. There is no sign to mark this area. You just have to know about it. One person can whisper into the corner and the person standing in the opposite corner will be able to hear them perfectly well because of the acoustics. Quite a neat little trick!

17. Eat REAL NY Pizza

Every few blocks you will find another pizza place to try. If you are in a neighborhood that you don't know, stop a local and ask for their favorite place. Every ten blocks or so, people will identify with *"their go to"* place for pizza. The great thing about New York is that you can buy it by the slice. Be sure to order it New York style which is very thin. Don't get weirded out when they hand it to you on a paper plate and stuffed in a brown bag. That's the New York way! A few noteworthy spots are Grimaldi's, Patsy's Pizzeria and John's of Times Square.

18. Find the Secrets of The Plaza Hotel

You may find yourself at the famous Plaza Hotel after strolling Fifth Avenue. The historic hotel has been featured in movies such as *Home Alone 2, Crocodile Dundee, Scent Of A Woman* and *Bride Wars*. This luxury hotel is a majestic site from the outside but did you know you can go inside even if you aren't staying there? There is a large entryway that is open to the public and is beautiful year round but stunning during the Christmas season. You can pay to have breakfast in this area as a non-resident of The Plaza. There is also a food court in the basement that is open to everyone. Walk right in like you belong because you do!

19. Be A Local At The Street Fairs

As a local to Manhattan, I always loved the milder seasons of spring and summer time for many reasons. These seasons allow for no more puffy coats, hats, gloves, boots and snow to walk through as you rush to the train for warmth. One other thing I enjoyed most about these warm months are the street fairs that would pop up around the city on Sundays. I would take my time running errands while weaving in and out of the booths. I would find anything from nail polish to organic honey to luxury sheets to international spices. You can try unique eats and some neighborhood restaurants and shops will put tables and merchandise outside for purchase. You can also find cool New York t-shirts that aren't too touristy. Check online for what neighborhood they will be in next weekend.

20. Don't Skip Lincoln Center

Even if you don't have the opera or ballet tickets for your trip, be sure to visit Lincoln Center. It is particularly beautiful at dusk and just after sunset. There is a beautiful fountain and a grass-roofed restaurant where you could have a lovely picnic or read a book. You will also be just next to the Julliard School of Arts. Keep in mind that there are certain times during the year that in the area outside of Lincoln Center, around the gorgeous lite fountain, they will host free *al fresco* shows. Look up "Met Summer HD Festival" to find out the next series. Also, there is typically a stand where they sell delicious gelato. This is a true New York experience and completely free!

Amy A. Sylvestre

"If Louis was right, and you only get one great love,

New York just may be mine."

Carrie Bradshaw

Amy A. Sylvestre

21. Bring Cash to Try the Best Street Food

There is so much competition in New York in every arena. It doesn't matter what you do or what shop you want to open. There is one already open and ready to compete. In midtown you will see street carts with all different types of dishes. The competition stops with *The Halal Guys* on West 53rd Street and Sixth Avenue. You will smell their delicious food before you see them and if you go at lunch time, you will see the line of locals around the block. The line is much more manageable at night. It's a lot of delicious food for one person. Bring cash and enjoy.

22. Don't Buy The Expensive Stuff

Inevitably you might need to buy something you forgot to pack. Don't get stuck paying the high tourist prices for a jacket, umbrella or scarf. Be on the lookout for the many *Housing Works* locations to find gently used items for a reduced price. You just might find a designer item donated by a famous neighbor. There are also Goodwill's around the city, and while cheaper than other shops, the prices will likely be more expensive than your Goodwill or thrift store back home.

23. Visit The Highline

Some creative, talented people with big ideas saw the vision of turning the old elevated New York Railroad into a lovely city park called *The Highline*. Often you will find musicians performing, benches where you can take a rest, yummy ice cream and unique places to take photos of the city below. Also, stop for lunch or a treat at the neighborhood staple, *The Standard Grill*. Nearby you will find *The Chelsea Market* with many places to eat and shops like *Anthropologie*, *Amy's Bread* and *Doughnuttery*. This is a good rainy day activity as well but this area can easily get quite crowded.

24. Don't Miss The Best Burgers & Shakes

There are so many places in Manhattan for delicious burgers. You'll find different takes on this American classic meal as you find burgers with added bacon, avocado, pimento cheese and even more adventurous toppings. In my opinion, the very best burger in the city is found at *The Shake Shack*. This burger joint has had so much success that in the last decade it has spread around Manhattan and even to other major cities in the United States. The original location is in Madison Square Park. Here they offer outside seating with amazing views of the Flatiron building, a triangular skyscraper built in 1902. This is a great area to explore with a neat atmosphere and great shopping. If you are looking for more than a burger, check out Eataly Market for a unique experience. If it is cold out, don't skip the unmatchable hot chocolate at The City Bakery. If you decide on that delicious burger from the *Shake Shack*, be sure to also enjoy a concrete or a shake. You will need to go to the West 77th location to order the "Upper West Slide," which is my favorite.

25. Eat A Meal On The Hudson

If you enter Riverside Park at West 72nd street, head south along the river to *Pier i* Café for a burger or hot dog. You can sit at the café tables or take your food out on the pier for a picnic on a blanket or the benches over The Hudson. You will have a prime view of sail boats, New Jersey and the helicopter tours above you. If you prefer to go north at West 72nd Street, you can take a nice walk and enjoy a meal at the open air restaurant called the *Boat Basin*. It is such an interesting location that offers seating with views of the scenic Hudson River. Both of these destinations are best for sunny days without rain.

26. Remember In Lower Manhattan

Where were you on September 11, 2001? We all remember how that day happened for each of us. After many years of planning, researching and building, the city has done an excellent job creating a memorial for 9/11. You can visit the site where the World Trade Center once stood and see the majestic fountain with the names of the victims as well as the Freedom Tower. St. Paul's Cathedral is next to the memorial and the nearby museum is always free. There are other sites to see in this area. It is a great place to go and remember how our brave nation has recovered and pay respects to those we lost. Never forget!

27. Bike Along The Hudson

If you truly want to be among the locals, take a walk or go for a bike ride along the Hudson River next to Riverside Park. You can easily rent bikes around the city through *Citi Bike* with your credit card. Head north towards the George Washington Bridge that connects Manhattan to New Jersey. You will find the lovely Little Red Lighthouse in Fort Washington Park just below the bridge. This historic lighthouse was built in 1889. The area along the Hudson brings such a relaxing break and welcomed relief to the hustle and bustle of the city. You might be the only tourist around because very few folks visiting the city take the time to explore this area. Also, don't be fooled that Paris is the only city of love. Walking hand in hand in this picturesque area of Manhattan, will make your heart skip a beat. As Robert De Niro shared, "I go to Paris, I go to London, I go to Rome, and I always say, "There's no place like New York.

It's the most exciting city in the world now. That's the way it is. That's it." You will start to see and understand why people choose to live in New York after spending some time along The Hudson River. On a personal note, I named my second son, Hudson, for this amazing river where I often would take walks with his daddy.

28. Visit Top Of The Rock Or Empire State Building

I'm sure you've seen a movie like, *Sleepless in Seattle* or the classic*, An Affair to Remember*, that uses the historic Empire State Building as not just a backdrop but part of the storyline. This 102-story skyscraper is more majestic in person than in any movie you've seen. The views of the city below surpassed my expectations and you can take breathtaking photos from every direction. Be aware that if you have trouble standing for long periods of time that the lines are long and there aren't places to sit. If you don't have the time or finances to go to both the Rockefeller Center and the Empire State Building, consider that if you go to "Top of the Rock," you can get pictures of the city including the Empire State Building.

29. See A Movie In Bryant Park

If you enjoy seeing people in their natural habitat, Bryant Park is a great place to hang out during the work week. This is a place that locals come for a meal and to soak up the sun. You can even write a quick email or look up another site to visit on the free wifi offered here. Because of its location, you will see true New Yorkers taking a break from long work days. You can also walk around the block and stop in the beautiful New York City Library. Check online for a schedule of when free movies are shown in Bryant Park. You can also periodically do yoga or ice skate with the locals depending on the weather in this favorite city spot.

30. Try Some Spice With Indian Food Under the Lights

If you enjoy spice as much as I do, don't miss this one of kind restaurant called *Panna II*. This is a true New York experience where you have a bit of hassle but it is worth it in the end. You will more than likely be surrounded by locals who have the scoop on neat places to check out. There will most definitely be a wait outside on the sidewalk, no matter what the weather is, and the restaurant is quite small. They serve yummy Indian Food but are known for their atmosphere. The neat photos of all the lights throughout the tiny restaurant will make for great pictures to post of your unique find in Manhattan. Beware that they only take cash. Call ahead.

Amy A. Sylvestre

"Manhattan is basically this island in New York,

where all the cool stuff is located."

Jason Medina

Amy A. Sylvestre

31. Take the Staten Island Ferry

If you are own a budget, taking the Staten Island Ferry is a great way to get a decent view of the Statue of Liberty without paying for the actual trip to Liberty Island. You can take the Staten Island Ferry FREE of charge. The trip coming back to Manhattan from Staten Island will offer you amazing views of the famous New York City skyline with the new Freedom Tower. The Ferry runs every day, all day but be sure to check the schedule for your ride over and back. The trip from lower Manhattan's South Ferry stop to Staten Island's Whitehall Ferry Terminal will take just under half an hour.

32. People Watch In Union Square

You will find many eclectic folks hanging out in Union Square. There are students, professionals and artists all occupying the same space. Sit for a few minutes on the benches or steps and take in a crowd of people from all over the world. There is a fabulous farmers market here full of locals called the Greenhouse Market. It is worth checking out. This area is also a place where people will gather to voice their opinions in civil protests. I really enjoy this neighborhood in the evening and is a great place to grab your dinner and hang out. One thing to make note of, is if walk through this area, there are the strange changing numbers that most people can't figure out. This exhibit is called the *Union Square Metronome*. The best explanation I've found says, "The 15 numbers of the digital clock display time going and coming relative to midnight. Read time going left to right and time coming in the opposite direction. So, if the clock reads

070437000235616 it means that it is 7:04 A.M. (7 hours and 04 minutes since midnight) and that there are 16 hours, 56 minutes and 23 seconds remaining until midnight. The three numbers in between are a blur of moving numbers."

Hopefully this explanation will save you some confusion and a long conversation with all the tourists standing around and debating its meaning.

33. Run The City

New York is full of runners. People go running, have running parties, talk about running, organize races and will share their PR's (personal records) readily. There are races held in Central Park throughout the year and many of them are hosted by New York Road Runners. Pack your shoes and sign up for one of their races before your trip. You won't regret it! The loop of the park is just over six miles and includes some famous sites and some hills that will test your athletic skills. If you are in the city during the end of October and the first weekend in November, you will see advertisements and signs for the New York City Marathon. Running is in the air during this season and it is an incredible event to witness it firsthand. The downside is that some roads are closed during the days before the race and the crowds around Central Park make getting around more difficult. Good luck!

34. Venture North

In Manhattan there is so much to see south of West 59th street that you could easily not experience the upper part of the borough. I would encourage you not to miss out on the tasty street tacos in Spanish Harlem or the beautiful parts at the tip of Central Park. If you need a glimpse of suburban life, you will also find the only *Target* in upper Manhattan. You will enjoy a walk on Amsterdam Avenue from West 86th street down to West 77th Street. There are so many restaurants with cool vibes with outdoor seating. Go further north and check out the beautiful *The Cloisters* museum in Fort Tryon Park. The grounds around the museum are something to see! If you take the time to venture further north, you will also find the last remnant of the forest that once covered Manhattan in *Inwood Park*.

35. Unwind At Music Bars

If you enjoy live music and dancing, you will enjoy getting a drink at the local Upper West Side bar, *Prohibition*. They often have extremely talented cover bands perform and you can enjoy your night by dancing and singing along with a crowd of locals. You can also venture down to the super hip Lower East Side and dance the night away at *Pianos*. If you are up for late night music and dancing, don't believe the name of this bar called, *No Fun*. Be safe, take a friend and have a blast!

36. Everyone Has to Go Some Time

Within a few hours of touring this amazing city, you will realize that it is difficult to find restrooms when you need one. Many stores and restaurants will lock their restrooms and expect a purchase to open it. Your best bet is to look for a Starbucks, McDonald's or even a large clothing store. The Upper East Side is largely residential and it is quite difficult to find public restrooms. Fifth Avenue can also be a challenge. You can find public toilets but it isn't easy. There is a restroom near Bethesda Fountain and also near the Great Lawn and theater in Central Park. A convenient place "to go" is in the Apple Store on East 59th Street and 5th Avenue. A huge help is that they are open 24 hours a day. The most elegant *potty* you may find in New York is in The Plaza Hotel.

37. Explore The Ramble

If you want to forget the noise of the city, take a long walk through *The Ramble* in Central Park. You will feel like you are on a hike in the mountains and not in the middle of a huge city. You might even be able to avoid all the car horns and police sirens for a few minutes! *The Ramble* is a wonderful escape from big city living. It is located slightly west in the park and you can find it easily from the west 77th entrance. Just cross the beautiful bridge with picturesque views of the water and city then enter a world most tourists miss out on. You can find a rock to read on or sit with a friend by the water. It is also a romantic, quiet place to avoid the crowds. You may be one of the few visitors who will find his or her way into the special part of the park. Enjoy the quiet and space!

38. Take A Taxi

You might have the Uber app on your phone but the easiest way to get a ride in NYC is still the yellow taxi. Just raise your hand and one will stop in seconds. Taxi's calculate their fairs based on time and not mileage. If the light on the roof is not on then they are off duty or already have a passenger. Keep in mind that taxi drivers change their shift from 3:30pm to 4:30pm and it can be challenging to hail a cab around these times, particularly in Midtown. Rush hour and rainy days are also more challenging. Give yourself more time. There is an understanding that you don't' hail a cab right next to someone else hailing a cab. Go to the next corner, wait until they get in their taxi or prepare to fight. Remember what Johnny Carson told us about taking a taxi, "Anytime four New Yorkers get into a cab without arguing, a bank robbery has just taken place."

39. Don't Miss The West Village

The Village is a quieter neighborhood than most. Stop in for some nice, smooth jazz at a restaurant bar called, "The Garage." Enjoy delicious French food on West 11th and West 4th at *Tartine*. Be sure to order the spicy chicken with guacamole and fries. You can also bring your own bottle of wine here. After dinner you can stroll down to the original *Magnolia Bakery* for delicious cupcakes. If you love the show, *Friends*, you can stop at Monica and Rachel's apartment on the corner of Grove Street and Bedford Street. John Lennon of the Beatles shows his love for New York when he said, "I regret profoundly that I was not an American and not born in Greenwich Village. It might be dying, and there might be a lot of dirt in the air you breathe, but this is where it's happening."

0. Buy Groceries

Eating out every meal will add up quickly no matter where you are visiting but in New York it can seriously get out of hand. You can easily find *bodegas* (small stores) on street corners but their prices will be higher for the convenience. Your best bet for your budget is *Trader Joes*. They promise to keep their prices the same nationwide. There is also *Fairway* and *Whole Foods* but the prices are typically higher. If you pass an outdoor fruit and vegetable stand at night, stop! The prices are dirt cheap! I've gotten whole bags of salad for a dollar as well as pound of grapes or a box of strawberries for a dollar. You will need cash. Best of luck with staying on budget!

Amy A. Sylvestre

"New York is not a city. It's a world."

B. Brown

Amy A. Sylvestre

41. Get Your Show Tickets Here

Some people come to New York simply for the experience of the musicals on Broadway. Your best bet for reduced price tickets is to go to Times Square to TKTS. You can also attempt to win the lottery for particular shows. You will have to go online to see when the lotteries are held and what rules you must follow. Most lotteries will require you are present when they draw the numbers to claim your tickets. I hope you win! You can also go to the box office and see if there are standing room only or single tickets that are not together for a reduced rate. Many theaters will offer discounts for those with a student id or senior citizens. You can also venture out and see an off Broadway show for much cheaper. Enjoy the show!

42. Take Your Best Shots Here

A simple picture of the city streets full of yellow taxi cabs can make for an interesting picture. Pretty much everywhere you look, there is something new to capture. But, there are a few spots that offer unique views. Be sure to get a picture from the bridge right outside of The Ramble in Central Park. Don't miss the shot from Brooklyn Bridge with the city skyline behind you. You can also get great shots of Lincoln Center from the bar on the roof of Empire Hotel. There is typically no cover fee for entrance to this bar. Go to the Castle in Central Park to capture Turtle Pond and the Great Lawn. On the far north side of the Great Lawn, you will see the city scape with the greenery of the park together. It is gorgeous! Take a walk around the Reservoir and you can get a great shot of the opposite side of the city. On the west side of the park from the famous Bow Bridge, you will also seeing the west side buildings as the backdrop to the turtle pond. Just gorgeous!

43. Indulge In The Best & Heaviest Cookies

Give in to your sweet tooth at *Levain Bakery*! It is a very small shop and easy to miss. Be on the lookout on West 74th and Amsterdam for a cute little bench and blue trimmed door. There are quite a few delicious choices at this tiny bakery but I would suggest getting their signature treat, a chocolate chip cookie with walnuts. Plus, they serve it warm! To save a bit of money, get your milk at one of the bodegas on the corner on Amsterdam. I bet you have to take a bite within minutes of buying it. You might even surprise yourself and finish the whole thing! It is worth every calorie.

44. Explore Peruvian Eats

Pio Pio is a restaurant that offers family style meals with delicious roasted chicken. I would suggest getting the Matador Combo served with avocado, salad, rice, beans and ask for the sweet plantains. This meal will easily feed two to three people. They are also known for their bright red sangria and reasonable prices. They offer several signature seafood dishes as well. Whichever dish you decide to order, be sure to ask for extra green sauce because it makes the meal! They have several Manhattan locations but my favorite is on Amsterdam.

45. Be Festive

Manhattan is always an amazing place to visit but there are certain times of year that it is a breath-taking place to be. The Christmas season is simply gorgeous and at moments, feels like you are walking through a movie set. Lights, snow and decorations are all around you. It is like the lights of the city shine brighter this time of year. This special festive season begins in November to be ready for the Macy's Thanksgiving Day Parade. In addition to Christmas, you can visit the Macy's store for their world renown flower show in the spring near the Easter season. In the fall, the Lower East side hosts a spectacular parade for Halloween. The Independence Day fireworks on the 4th of the July, light up the sky over the Hudson River. Find a pier and have a picnic. The show starts at sunset!

46. Enjoy The Seasons

It is certainly easier to get around New York when it is nice weather. In the milder months, locals shed their puffy coats, eat most their meals outside and choose walking over the subway. But, don't avoid the city during the rest of the year. The changing seasons are beautiful to experience. The leaves in the fall in Central Park will make a lasting impression. A new snow will bring a quiet newness to the city before it all turns black a few days later. Even still, spring and summer tend to be most locals' favorite. These seasons offer free music in the park, more daylight to roam the city and movies on the Hudson.

47. Connect Spiritually

You might be surprised that there is a thriving population of people of faith in Manhattan. There are so many interesting people with different views on spirituality, faith and religion all living together seeking truth and freedom. Take a break from the busyness of touring and check out one of these services to connect spiritually. If you want unbelievable worship, stop in for a service at *Hillsong*. If you want to hear teaching that will change your life, stop in at one of the three locations for *Redeemer Presbyterian Church*. Another great community of faith is *Trinity Grace Church* and they also offer services around the city. You won't be disappointed hanging out with locals at any of these services. Many offer services throughout the day on Sunday and not just in the morning. Also, most offer free snacks and coffee!

48. Step Into Wonderland

If you are traveling with children, Alice's Tea Cup is such a cute place for a meal or a treat. They will offer the little ones fairy wings and tiaras to wear while you enjoy huge delectable scones drizzled with a sweet sauce. Be sure to get the pumpkin scone, even if it is out of season. Don't skip the jam and cream! Adults enjoy this unique restaurant just as much as the kiddos for the delicious food, lovely atmosphere and afternoon tea. There are two locations in Manhattan.

49. Learn To Brunch

New Yorkers are experts at many things and one of those things is how to brunch. It is common among locals to talk about brunch, go to brunch for hours and compare brunch locations. Weekend brunch lasts all morning through the afternoon and often until 4pm. You can find some amazing brunch dishes at "Good Enough to Eat," "Cilantro," "Sara Beth's," "Balthazar," "Café Mogador," and "The Smith." Don't pass up the chance to enjoy steak and eggs in a city that loves "*to brunch*."

50. Don't Do Too Much

While living in Manhattan, friends from outside the city would comment that they could never live in such a busy place. They would tell me about their three day trip to New York and how exhausting and hard it was to get around. They left with a bitter taste in their mouths. While I understand their experience, I love New York. There are hard aspects to life in *The City* but the benefits outweigh the costs. If you are coming for a short trip, don't overextend yourself. Pick a day to run around and be a tourist. Balance it with leisurely walk along the Hudson or East River. Then, hit the ground running the next day with some major tourist attractions but then end your vacation with a long, slow walk in one of the amazing city parks. Pick a good spot and give yourself time to people watch and just soak up the beauty and the chaos together. You'll join the rest of us locals who say, "I love New York" and you can proudly rock your heart t-shirt back in your hometown. Bon Voyage!

Amy A. Sylvestre

Top Reasons to Book This Trip

- **The Food:** You can enjoy food from all of the world within just a few blocks. Savor a new place every meal!

- **The Energy:** While city life can be exhausting, there is a buzz in the air and even after long work weeks, people will be out and about taking in all the city has to offer. Jump in with the locals!

- **The Pace:** A New York minute really is the shortest minute of all. In just a few days in the city that never sleeps, you will conquer more than any other place you visit. Have a blast!

Amy A. Sylvestre

> TOURIST

GREATER THAN A TOURIST

Visit GreaterThanATourist.com
http://GreaterThanATourist.com

Sign up for the Greater Than a Tourist Newsletter
http://eepurl.com/cxspyf

Follow us on Facebook:
https://www.facebook.com/GreaterThanATourist

Follow us on Pinterest:
http://pinterest.com/GreaterThanATourist

Follow us on Instagram:
http://Instagram.com/GreaterThanATourist

Amy A. Sylvestre

> TOURIST

GREATER THAN A TOURIST

Please leave your honest review of this book on Amazon and Goodreads. Thank you.

We appreciate your positive and negative feedback as we try to provide tourist guidance in their next trip from a local.

> TOURIST

GREATER THAN A TOURIST

Our Story

Traveling is a passion of the "Greater than a Tourist" series creator. Lisa studied abroad in college, and for their honeymoon Lisa and her husband toured Europe. During her travels to Malta, an older man tried to give her some advice based on his own experience living on the island since he was a young boy. She was not sure if she should talk to the stranger but was interested in his advice. When traveling to some places she was wary to talk to locals because she was afraid that they weren't being genuine. Through her travels, Lisa learned how much locals had to share with tourists. Lisa created the "Greater Than a Tourist" book series to help connect people with locals. A topic that locals are very passionate about sharing.

Amy A. Sylvestre

> TOURIST

GREATER THAN A TOURIST

Notes